Watermark

Watermark

Jacquelyn Pope

WINNER OF THE
MARSH HAWK PRESS POETRY PRIZE, 2004

MARSH HAWK PRESS
EAST ROCKAWAY, NEW YORK
2005

First Edition
05 06 7 6 5 4 3 2 1

Marsh Hawk Press books are published by Poetry Mailing List, Inc.,
a not-for-profit corporation under section 501 (c) (3)
United States Internal Revenue Code.

Cover and interior design: Claudia Carlson
Author photo: Don Share
Cover map courtesy Harvard Map Collection, Harvard College Library

I would like to thank Marie Ponsot; Sharon Dolin,
Sandy McIntosh and Claudia Carlson; and Rita Gabis.
Special thanks to Jennifer Barber for reading and encouraging this book
from its earlier versions. And thanks above all to Don Share
for his indefatigable and irreplaceable support.

Library of Congress Cataloging-in-Publication Data

Pope, Jacquelyn.
Watermark / Jacquelyn Pope. — 1st ed.
p. cm.
Includes bibliographical references.
ISBN 0-9759197-2-5
I. Title.
PS3616.O654W38 2005
811'.6 — dc22

2004016824

Marsh Hawk Press
P.O. Box 206
East Rockaway, New York 11518-0206
www.marshhawkpress.org

for the girl who went out in the dark

Acknowledgements

Grateful acknowledgement is made to the editors of the following magazines, in which these poems appeared:

Agni: "Mrs. Robinson"
Alaska Quarterly Review: "In the Other Tongue"
Elixir: "Woman in Translation", "Number 17, the
   Shipbuilder's"
Gulf Coast: "In the Bonehouse", "There and Back"
Harvard Review: "Dwelling", "Watermark"
Indiana Review: "All Said and Done"
Literary Imagination: "Holiday", "World's End"
The Literary Review: "Cloud Reading"
Mystic River Review: "Sunday's Hours"
The New Republic: "Persephone Descending"
Partisan Review: "Gramarye", "Street of Endless Prayer"
Poetry: "Alice, After"
Puerto del Sol: "Benediction"
Salamander: "Household Economy", "Letter in Two
   Drafts", "Rain Diary"
Shenandoah: "Hoogstraat"
Southern Poetry Review: "A Lost Address"
Southern Review: "From a Crooked Wall" (as "In Time")

I preferred to see it in the distance, the blue, the treacherous, tremendous sea.

— JEAN RHYS, *Smile Please*

Contents

I.

II.

III.

I.

Raddled

Pieced together:

A shape, a space, a shadow —
    bruise of a buttonhole,
        the gap where I gather.

Fingered, frayed, futile
    I unravel, easy-as-you-please.
        Now ribbon and rush amend me
            stitched in time, tenses shuttled.

Impending, intending, I set to work
    as if thimble and bone
        would brace me, bear me out.

Alice, After

I should be glad for the roof,
shuddering with rain,
for the wool pulled warm
over my eyes. I should be
glad for the old walls
that keep me inside—
but I want to be sweet-talked
into something else,
want to be surprised.
I'm careful, keep the curtains drawn,
all afternoon, the lights switched off,
though if anybody looked
they could see me through a crack,
fingers working to win
my body back. I go knock-kneed
like this, I'm tongue-tied,
a giantess who tears
through attic eaves, topples
chimney pots, unbending
in the weather's glaze.
I've grown weary of charms,
except for sleep. I should
stretch out far as I'm allowed,
resume my indoor
life, my old disguise:
milk-white, reliable, contracted.

Street of Endless Prayer

Under the orange arch of autumn
the weather of another life

Days count themselves
in rust in moss in scales
in stand-up hours
beaten across a brown carpet

Street of tram tracks and soapsuds
alley of second guesses
city of wish-I-wanted
I've been weathering you
your light like praise
rise and fall, fall and rise
without a word from life

City of past persistence
I have a room in your walls
a house made of stone syllables
of dust and sleep

hope make this ruined house
a home hope salvage me

Woman in Translation

Weeks, months, seasons:
each darkness fit to paper,
cut to size. Mirror
in the window, make
a measure of me.
Lend me hope, hand
on heart, a folded fan,
a flower. Bitumen bloom,
my name at the end
of the letter. End of the year:
the streets are feathered,
red, fired out. Nothing I see
makes a sound. Let me
make a start. I will
stand in the middle,
rest in the middle,
root in the middle
of this soft fresh tide:
light striking glass,
the street's arc and clamor
as its spell of tones
converges and disappears,
folded into the wordless night.
I have fallen out of favor,
out of phrases, learned
the fluency of shadows
moving deeper, downward
in the dark. Let me
be written into this world:
something of substance
behind me now.

Hoogstraat

From a grey barge in brackish water
I watched summer come to flower, arched
and green. Bedclothes puffed from open
windows where the city aired its stuffy rooms.
Bicycles clicked by and a waiter weaved
between them, with a tray of white blooms —
bloemkool, I thought, cabbage roses, round
as the open mouths of the couple stopped to kiss
at the corner, sun glancing from their hair,
skin shining from the reckless heat.
Summer seemed as open, as empty as the street
that was my own, my sole horizon. Only water
came and went, and it took the light along,
out to the careless sea for a lilac drowning.

Dream on a Train

Drawn on a line
fixed to the future,
drawn to a point
pulled through a frame.
Drawn to the horizon,
destination deferred.

And by leaving, looking forward:
to ship lanes, sheared continents,
a mud-made plain of hardened shadows.

Cast out of time
blue broken by gold
marsh crusted by tides;
the wake of tracks and stations.

Intervals of sand
give way to fields turned by stone.
Ringroads circle exhausted towns,
streets bare between stations
where vault and echo hover,
abandoned idioms.

Borders, balconies, second thoughts.
The drift of smoke from chimneys.

Seasons, weathers, sunlight
pass through me —

Sea and salt air, boulevards
drained of summer heat. Chipped tiles,
lost tickets. Itinerant hours,
the swell of show tunes on an empty beach.

Now I am alive again
I forget everything I know —

Someone tells a story
that takes on another language.
Someone is bragging
in block letters, in stick figures.
Someone is whispering a prayer.

Solitary skies. A haze of sea
giving way, giving ground.

There's a line seeking to cross itself
pulled in all directions, scripting shadows
while the wind, seeking a way between
pillows a wash line,
changing direction, changing everything.

O

O   you are the only one
that's suited to my mouth.
O   you are my old reliable,
good as your word, even last in line.

O   you are the drum of rain
on the roof, the rasp
            of sorrow at the door,
the exclamation of skies.

O   you are the blue of tides,
your broad sails pillowing
            with wind. You come up
round as bells, slip clear of song.

O   you are the register
of leaving, longing after.

Rain Diary

I fog the window
in a rain-colored country
where the clouds are hurried,
incomprehensible.

In this season of shipwrecks and falling stars
gulls spread their pale wings, spiral the sky's tides.

Now settled like silt in my room,
I watch word after word
wash out of the rivermouth,
watch distance circling to disappearance.

Antiquarian

I opened a door in a dream
and the city became a book in my hands,
indexed by streets, bound
by tides. Doorways echoed

left and right, wind rushed
the riggings of brigs
and frigates, barges heaved
and sighed. Everywhere I walked

I heard the record of the air:
foreword and afterword,
muttering, shouting, prayer;
whispers, cries, sermons —

archived in layers, in a mortar
of wishes, dreams, decrees
encircling alleys, breaking
into squares where its years

were written as floods and plagues,
imagined as they disappeared.
The city's sentence came
from kings and clerics, bishops

and bricklayers, whores
and hangmen, nuns and spies.
Its story was written in backwash
and breaking water,

in the melancholic lines
of wharves, wires, ropewalks;
of cranes, domes, statues, spires
intruding on the air.

Brick and stone were its
gutter and spine. Page
by page the city
turned and told its trades

in places where water
speaks to wind and wind
to water, in signatures
of time and vanishings.

The Good Wife

Old book, old broom, a penny's pleasure;
stuff run in rings, around and round.
But rounder still: be light, be leavening,
true as time. You can't make a box
from a broken arrow. You can't keep
faith and flower. Pretty is as
pretty does, but pretty doesn't
do without. The rest make do. Tasked,
contrived, you've been left to gloom back,
bulk up the rear. In your fog heart,
from your faded eyes you're an exile,
confined to locked doors and lost time.

Elemental

From the roof, there's a view through rain, rush
and gully down the bends of gabled walls.
Steeples, spires needle a weave of clouds,
church bells slur out to sea. The streets are cinched
by the slush of cars, by the yellow bulk
of trams sent sighing down their tracks. It's July,
the seventh month of the seventh year
spent starting over. There's a brailled banknote
balled like a fist in my pocket, saved for
something I've forgotten. There's a smell
of damp and sinking, the sound of boats
groaning against their moorings, the look
of light broken from the dark. From the height
of summer, from anchors and fogs, time wrecked
and recirculated, there's a view through
grit and grey, a sense of something
starting, of a world kept shaded out of sight.

Dwelling

Home was two rooms, a crook of stairs,
a skylight shedding dust
in spiraled air. We spent weeks
in boxes and goodbyes
while nights deepened to cold squares,
bricked up on all sides.

I married his house, his family,
married struts and stone,
a rusting balcony, dark shapes
I learned with brush
and broom, rationed into rooms,
slipped understairs. And in the stilled
heart of home, the hallway's
secret damp seeped with age,
a radio was set to steady days
with broadcasts on the hour.

Under blankets, under beams
we sheltered by blank windows
tucked under roof tiles
and chimney stones, under
the briny air, its muddied stars.

Household Economy

Begin by paring back, by peeling down.
Learn by leaving out, by leaving the rest
for last, making certain it's forgotten.

(But keep a close account of all that's kept
unspoken. Preserve the strict routines
of shut-up rooms, where dust settles a scored

ledger of omissions.) Once the clock stalls,
while the mirror stammers, set out spoons
and cups to serve the evening's broth of scraps.

Keep the fire banked with rags and husks.
Cut down or turn out whatever wears out,
save your breath for shaping mending words.

The Baker's Wife

He would have me square
　　but I slip round
in slowed time stealing
　　his ash his soot his fire
turning to plump and soften
　　on the yeasty air

In the hot white cup
　　of marriage I dissolve
that's how I was made
　　what he took me for

I take the lift he leaves
　　over I take the lot
he leaves back all its
　　crust and salt all
the stuff that shapes
　　the forms between us
spice that sets the matter
　　before us preserved

until he wakes and sees
　　me warm risen
and of good crumb

Cloud Reading

The city exists where a snarl of cloud
is pierced through by church spires,
fretted by scaffolds, crowned with barbed wire.
Circular, medieval,
it would do away with stars,
heap dust and spice to declare ascendance.

The city exists in moats and crescents,
in darkening walls, a dusky sea
of roofs, the crest of gables.
The city exists where water
meets with water, forging jewelled light
to sway its masts and sails.

The city exists over time,
over bells and steeples, over channeled shadows.
Under wings, under the crowns
of trees, under the wind's mute sentence,
the city circles, tunnels on.

A Lost Address

Windows written by rain,
described by fog, by rusting weather.
Windows filling with the script
of another sluggish summer,
where drizzle sounds like misery
over the hand-me-down brick
of the broken-up *plein*.
A ring of darkened houses
huddles around the harbor, slipshod,
inclined toward chance
and distances, smudged
with the salt stain of the sea.
Here by the hearth fire
I keep my word,
high and dry. Bitter,
balanced, unspoken things
cling to dust and to dissolving.
It sounds like rain, and rain
sounds again and again in me.

Brief Season

Late August. The day lifts from dust,
from long greening. Water curves
and stalls, luminous. Wind scales
the quayside stairs. It roughens moss-
slicked walls, rocks dockbound boats,
their blank and slackened sails. A last
glance of sun circles barge straw
and bicycle spokes as evening turns:
water winds and slows, running comb-
toothed, sluiced, counter to shadow.
Crowds abandon trains. Human sounds
trickle and echo in fissures of green—
bottle glass, broken arch—as the station's
clockface whitens, keeping hours.

Red Scarf

The scarf is red and circles me like smoke. It is silk, broad and blank, the hem unravelled on one side. I found it lying in the gutter, mudsoaked. Once I washed the street out and it dried, it slipped soft warmth around my throat. Nothing else touched me. Red in my eyes, red drawing my mouth, the silk taste of the wind on a bicycle. I remembered the first sight of them, rounding a corner and the ribbons, the flags that followed. The secret film of it, black spokes and blue silk, the trill of bells like the racing fringe of a red scarf.

II.

Watermark

April balcony evening   spring's dark
curtain coming on   a deepening
blackdrop   the end of an act
I am eight weeks gone   I've come
years away   to stand up four
flights from   the water's wave
and angle   to watch it siphoned
into channels   grids of shadow
that draw me down   water parted
from rivers   parted from storm
wearied along an undercurrent
water whispers   to the water in me
tensed and balanced   trenches
defenses   city walls sidestreet
understreet   a tunneling line
crossed   double-crossed   underscored

Persephone Descending

Here in my lesser life I lie describing
the sun's sweep across a brilliant summer sky,
drawn up in such blue as I'm abandoned by.

It's conjured. Now I'm the slightest shadow
of his shadowed land,
stepchild, the light of his left hand.

Here I am kept and kept from.
I bloom like poison in my ration of air,
shuddering as his boots scrape down the stairs.

Seasons clutch and fade and I turn
frumpy and devout—I am forgotten,
forgetting how, here to look on

and nod surprise. He has the last look out.
From my cinder bed,
in my chill-for-bones, I am blind,

bound to his gloom. I lie
under oceans, under rivers, under rain
and dream the world out of the dark, regained.

Gramarye

Underdrawn,
I translate herb with root:
aromatic, darkened,
drawn together in a doubled cartouche.

Undermined,
I crawl the earth beneath the house,
watch heat fill cracks in the hardwood floor,
watch it pool, pull up and disperse.

Underscored,
my roots grow silver, lengthen and fracture.
A mix, a pinch, a press of darknesses
spun to waxen ligatures.

Underground,
I sieve the earth, save the rest:
all that is settled, parenthetical,
the glint and spark of what resists.

Number 17, the Shipbuilder's

The house leans. It lists
but does not grieve. The house
sways on its beams, backs a brick of days,
draws the dust down with blinds.

Deep in the cool, down in the dark,
deaf to the sea, the street,
where rooms run underground,
an undiscovered continent:

doors, drawers, cupboards,
pulleys and chains. Shores of brick
and plaster, braces of rust and iron,
the layered marks of tides.

With its red roof raised,
with white eaves crowning the distance,
the house sails, crossing borders
to plunge deep in blued gardens,
in the crest of a blackening sea.

In the Bonehouse

Such time I had, I spent alone,
sequestered in the small and cramping dark.
A stitch of skin gave shape
to the hollowed form I fit,
a corset of blood and salt.

My heart settled its scores,
whitened its muscle rib by rib.
I grew gristle and bone
out of air and iron,
out of the dust my lungs sucked in.

In time my tongue turned hard
and white, lathering soap
until my soap-mouth foamed
and sang, all fume and boil,
all hook and dazzle. Dumbstruck,

the scar formed,
out of scum and sinking,
drawn to edges, apprehensions.
Let it live in ash
and echo then, weathered by the dark.

Ghostlily

Lily my life in daylight
depends on the dark
where I am wedged and green
and my thrush mouth gapes
at stars.

      These are my hours.
I reach, root, descend:
tipping earthward, senses spiraled,
twining to my end. Down
I drive and from my depth
emerge: wrinkled, wrong-
side-out, rooted on the verge.

In the Interval

Five-past-half-seven: the days
boil down in cabbage dinners,
dog's years in dull hours,
twilight idling at the door.

A day long, a day short, a dead series
mounted on the calendar's page.
I do and I do: so I did
but nothing would do:

false hopes, false starts,
truth in brackets and broomstraw,
in the sideswipe of tomorrow
and tomorrow . . . Gin thimbles,

talk tumbles. I am half seen,
not heard, sworn to one who won't
accept a promise, til death
divide us, at the hour of not-just-yet.

Iris

Petal   petal
petal   part me there

I've put mud on
for spring   stalked straight

I lean left of shadow
into curls   colors sinking
soaking   see me round   ruffling open

Vagabond

Here you've got used to guesswork
and gesture, looking on blank

as you like, where nothing can say
what you are, where you're going,

where wind-tinted signs turn bends
in your mouth, songs for setting out,

for stringing along, circling a homeless
town, letting the day decide, making

up life in lost hours, left to the rain
and after, to the bright husk of air

hung over the street, the map
that leads you out, that leads you on.

Evening's Line

As it comes back, page by folded page,
I say to myself, strange I lived there,
walked those streets. Took the river road
on summer evenings — violet hovered
over listless water, resignation
idled in the air. Such was my first sight

of paradise: piss-marked, tobacco-stained,
a place for everything and everything
in place, *amen*. A ferry pushed across
the water, dragging its scrim of shadow,
inscribing the elaborated air:
as it is, so it was, and shall not change.

Parting from Shame

In life I led you by the hand, dragging you east
then west again, pinning my hopes on the horizon,

on any flutter of chance. For you I invented
costumes, postures, manners. I cultivated

accents, practiced surprise. I suffered
your intuitions, indulged your delays,

slogged through a sleep of routine. With you
I'd recite the world, emptied of things, washed of hope.

I gave you shelter, gave you wine and water,
sang you to sleep on a pallet of straw and hoaxes.

You stood me doubt or dreams — I never could decide.
Now weariness has weathered me. I see I've shifted

and survived you, though your smudge hangs close:
the spoiled edge of selves dissolving, my devoted old ghost.

In a Dry Season

The day came when I gave up second thoughts.
I gave you back to the climate
you came from. Months
of winter lay between us,
a kind of peace.

I shook off your seasons,
cleaned and trimmed
and traded in my loss,
bound to live without provisions.

When there was nothing left to be undone,
I kept to the dark, deadbolted.
The hum of my heart hung on,
an answer to the ether.

Anemone

Bloom, you are weak to me,
wild to me, woe to me — wind cutting my curved room,
silt of surprise.

Scar in the air,
I give you good and dark.
I take you with magic that's all thumbs,
make you the hunch that crowds my tongue —

bloom, you are all heart.

Lament of the Out-of-lander

So much time spent squeezing into corners
shaded to the wall wrapped in the wrong clothes
and the wrong expression singed with the scent
of sourmouth stuck with a smile from some
other story left right left feet shifting
into a start of some other kind

O fortune written for a future
in far-off hands that dear desired time
that tunnel out of town that long clear look
at something else a march of prayers
promises a list of nouns and verbs
weightless formless as everything else

Who could be imperative wound this way
and that in the humdrum the halfwit in
the backslap the slapdash playing catch-as-
catch-can knitting up names and passports
humming out hopes pawned off on promises

On a minute in a moment one day
a someday never started when the riddle
of manners is at last unravelled when
history would hold off so much time spent
mistaking time for trouble unregistered
unnoticed given up for gone somehow
a tick too slow too studied too careful
forever the one moved out of the way

Out of the will there is a word webbed
in the mouth laid out in another life
how do you say the thing gone blank and deep
except despite how do you live strange

By Light

Under an arc of soft lamplight
I watched your hand turn the pages
of a book translated from one
foreign tongue into another,
still quite foreign to me. Then you
shifted, leaning closer to the light
and for the first I saw the stranger
you were bound to stay — secret, for-
ever separate from me. I sat
in my own pool of light, still wholly
untranslated into rooms that had
learned you long ago. Our shadows
hovered on their walls, dark forms
drawn across the future. Time flickered,
fading from the room the night
I saw our boundaries were drawn.

Holiday

A week strung from days blank as postcards.

A sketch of time undone, done
otherwise. Hollow days hung
between a railway and a deep blue sea,
white sun squat above hotels and their streets.

Days random as the shingle
washed across the beach. Bright days
bound by dark shutters. Days in bodies borrowed
for the occasion: new breath in old beds,
books read by a streetlamp's spill,
wine drunk from toothbrush glasses.

Days exchanged for a stranger's house and habits,
bread and jam exotica, white birds
in wire cages. Days on buses
numbered for invented routines.
Days sounded out in practiced phrases.

Days drawn from the spare, slow, southern sky,
white as forgetting, white as
the promise that all is forgotten.

Mrs. Robinson

I think of you, across the continent,
Testing your smile that ripened in catastrophe
And wonderfully ready now for death.

— WELDON KEES

He's fixed her off the page, where she's
abandoned: mid-century,
semi-continental. Cold sunlight
stabs the medicated air.
Too bored except to sit
and suck the mentholated tip
of her malaise, she wonders
at the nerve that led him on.

Gone abroad with her ambition,
she sees him with the key
to a mildewed motel room
where he shrugs on anonymity,
shaves new angles on his face
and edges into the drift
of a West Coast afternoon,
smiling like an ad man at the Golden Gate.

Now her camel-colored nails
ratchet the table where she waits.
She turns the clock to face the wall,
her chair to face the waves
of soybean, sorghum — sometimes
she swears she sees him,
motioning, a beacon from the green,
hands cupped to his mouth
though his lips aren't moving.
Gold shudders through the stalks
and he's gone. Strange days.
She can't account for it — how she's
survived. The way he disappeared.

{ *41* }

Tulips

Swaybacked but standing
they drowse across the path —
blowsy with wind and sun,
turbans undone,
colors greying.

Black hearts blown open,
peeled to spider frills.
All their silks unspun,
given back to air:
death-arched, flourishing.

Furiouser and Furiouser

His fortune's fixed. Mine's the one
needs mending, molding,
a surrogate of sorts—
something borrowed, something blue,
something to settle blame on.

I've given him grief that has run its course,
run rampant, run a rage,
spooned from the sugar bowl.
You have to have a hand in hope—
even the nag who sits home squandered,
nothing to scold.

On a day begged from the future,
bargained from his hoard,
I'll swing out, tipsy and shifting,
beggared by my rounds
and the curse of cowardice.

I'll shuffle through town
damp as a dull breeze, run at the hem.
I could be knotted, all knife blade
and tourniquet, the choke
of the chain and weight of the sack,
be the death of him: how dear,
how dark of me.

III.

Convergence

The sky and its cloud shores tumble and darken.
Night stoops under its burden of stars.
The hour's heart is still unbroken
though stalled, shamed
shunned into stone.

In the Other Tongue

It is a doorless house
on a whitened hill.

It is an upright chair
square in the windpath.

It is a still life
with bread and knife

in honey and brine,
a slow, dark region

of its own. Letter
by letter, long after,

a drift of vowels.
One word nestles

in another, turns
to fugitive things.

From the Album

Here is our secondhand house.

These are our worn-down days,
our love-on-loan.

Here I am, keeping to corners,
stained by winter,
slow to take hold.

There you are, soured
but sitting upright,
the beat of your breath
under lock and key.
You won't look at me.

And this was the last time light
moved through the page—
it emptied to gutters,
bound the book we made.

Goodbye to All That

Goodnight, goodbye,
I undo all I've said and done,

this life unlived, depending,
all the evenings spent upstanding

(wallflower, dormouse, doorflower)
given the same going-over

no matter how scarce, withdrawn.
No matter the shifts from side

to side, the sworn elisions,
swallowed sighs: they read me

the riot act, loud-mouthing words
I learned by heart. And learned

it's luck like this, disguised
as luck, that's led to life

in corners, days declined.
Now my days are done for —

I turned, X'd them aside. Time's
worn through, and I've resigned.

Sea-Leveled

Nothing to declare. A worn spot
on a hard seat, the highway
tunneling through fog
and a rain-bright land
parceled out to sea.

Unaccustomed gravities:
a spartan table
set for tea, sun threshed
through cloud then
splintered into gold.

Stone circles, encircles
the steepled, fading air.
The light of day slips
under bridges, after walls.
Widowed houses list

toward water, their windows
overlook the layering tide.
The city's claimed,
reclaimed by darkness —
and we've been settled under stars.

Sunday's Hours

I am numb as the bricks, dumb as the bells
in-between hours. Reading the wind's script

on the alley wall, watching the garden
grow its shadows, lying still. I'm still

as streaming water, still as the straits
running under our bed, and I swear

some cast-off cargo rusts and rattles there,
thick with the silt of Sunday's hours.

Letter in Two Drafts

Now the wind sends a scent of the sea,
of your grey island, marooned
in its course of tides.
Now the world is white storm.
This is the weather I answer you by.

Go on, shade.
I haven't touched you
since this time began,
haven't heard your voice.
You wouldn't stick by the likes of me,
but you do, you do.

Speak up, sky.
Night is a net that casts out stars.
Now this is the riddle I live by:
I asked for hope, and no hope came,
and grew familiar, a shape
that stayed beside me.

Such questions come,
falling on brick and pavement stone.
I've settled with dust
and disbelief. I'm home.

First Lesson in Silence

Thinking in circles   walking rings
a path between the fence   the moat
the wall   in steps beyond
the stuttering street   on stairs

Shuffled after corners   after shuttered
cafes   leaving out   leaving off
left to rumor   butcher   baker
bookseller   sorted in dark display

Caught in the mirror of the air
clear as water   clear as fire
clear as the stroke of cold come to cover
clear as the bells   ghosting this hour

All Said and Done

I had a mast and a crow's nest, a bright hint of the sea.

There were few stars on the grid of days,
long seasons of bread and salt, of folded newspaper.

I learned the cost of keeping peace,
loving winter for its perfect camouflage,
for all it used, used up and wore out.

I had maps fixed by memory,
by the scent of rain and brick,
but I lost that country:

its ink falls out of books you left behind.
These days, I do not do; I do without.

SRO

I stood in the half-light
of a near-hotel,
in the draft of its
comings and goings,
half hoping for home
(that destination fixed
by stars). Mutinous,
down-and-out, pursued
by doubt (well: bullied
into it), I'd come to claim
rest or resignation.
The lobby sagged on soured
chairs. A crook-backed man took
money, waved a finger
at the stairs. I had
five flights on the new world,
a cubbyhole where
I came to on a mattress
of night sweats and bedsores,
lights out all around,
night strangling on dead air
and dark sounds, on the breathless
heat of a homeless crowd.
Sirens, supplicants,
angels, accidents:
inquisitions were leveled
all around. Love had been
hungered and handed over.
I'd been declared: bewildered
as the rest, with the least
of life used, used up,
refused, with grief gone barren.

Forgetting How

I forgot the time, and time gave way
to seasons fluttered down a spike of or-
phaned Sundays. So I forgot my age,

lost my old breeze, the simplest sleights of hand.
I forgot my keys. I changed direction
on the hour, lost my wits and wondered where

my manners went, in spendthrift time, in time
spent pleasing, anxious, casting straws for cares
or cause, consigned to shame, to indecision.

Sum of soft parts, I was an anger
of muscle and bone, blind as bare hands,
a remnant pulled up and put down again.

Time cured me past caring. It left the lot,
day by day, box by box, withered at last
into forgetting, tangled in full stop.

Abroad

The habit ungrown is
grown apart: missing the shape,

the shade of permanence,
absent the spice of songs

of consolation. It is a last wish
worn through the ground,

spike in the dust, regeneration.
Undone is a ghost place.

Wedded to the dark, to drifts
of sleep, time's kept in fragments,

phrases, in crawl spaces
buried at the bottom of these days.

From a Crooked Wall

I heard the house around me
like an old familiar body,
a shell of shine and damp.

In bones I moved through its rooms,
through storms, second thoughts.
I watched it shift, separate in seams —

wall to floor to ceiling. It settled me.
Shifted from sight, from seeming,
I lived from phrase books and fading air.

Unpacking those hours,
I remembered their gifts, and the work
that made me: mixing flour, mending home,

putting words by. Now I am
wind-grown, gone from that grave,
though in dreams its dark pulse

still slips through mine and I
step back through its rain and ruin,
sure of my place each time.

Benediction

Wide from the world, I give you back to time:
back to the dark vault of summer, green arches,
linden canopies, fountains glinting
with castoff wishes, coins sunk for luck.
I give you back to black bubble taxis
beetling down brick-lined streets, to carved doors
opening on hushed white galleries
where orchestras set idle angles
in the afternoon air. I give you back
to wind-torn walks through town, to the sudden,
sobering cold of approaching storm.
I give you gold, the light-struck horizon,
the sink and swerve of gulls pursuing
ferries, flags snapping down the straitened course
of an inland sea. I give you that sea
and its surrounding, a prospect of the past,
a shelter for you, simply gone from me.

There and Back

I am the only one
who walks these streets,
slow-motioned. The world
streaks past in cars.

The ground gives way,
one step at a time
on this edge of old
bottles, bones. Rutted,

underslung, it trails off
and on, thickens
as it banks the asphalt's curve.
I ask the pines
for news of home.

I believe the grass,
the crows, the vines,
I believe the clinging heat:
there's a wish, a will,
a way, a hundred others;

there's a backlife,
an afterlife, a life
that comes from the ruin
of fire, threading a crevice,
pushing past stone.

World's End

One day I shall walk out and cross the sea
and crossing it shall carry me from tides
below the oyster shell of sea meeting sky
and I shall come up on the other side—
back of beyond, a land covered with frost,
studded with fires. I'll have a hearth for home,
bundle in blankets, locked up, alone.
Rainbeaten door, shadow-deepened frame,
I'll pace from door to mirror, back again,
the water beyond me silent, unseen,
shiftless as I was ever meant to be.
From a shoal of strange faces, odd stares
will wash toward me, and drown, for I'll be
adrift at last—salt-strewn, cold as they come,
I'll come alive in the wrack of the sea.

Notes

"Hoogstraat" – *bloemkool* is cauliflower

"A Lost Address" – *plein* is a public square

"Mrs. Robinson" – the epigraph is from Weldon Kees, "Poem Instead of a Letter"

"Benediction" – "wide from the world" is from Hart Crane, "Interior"

About the Author

PHOTO BY: DON SHARE

JACQUELYN POPE was educated at the University of Minnesota and Boston University. Her poems, reviews, essays and translations have appeared in journals and newspapers in the United States and Europe. Her writing has received the José Marti Prize and awards from the Academy of American Poets and the Massachusetts Cultural Council. She lived in The Netherlands for seven years, where she worked as a bookseller and translator. She currently lives in Dedham, Massachusetts with her husband and their daughter.

Other Books
from Marsh Hawk Press

GOSSIP, Thomas Fink
ARBOR VITAE, Jane Augustine
BETWEEN EARTH AND SKY, Sandy McIntosh
THE POND AT CAPE MAY POINT, Fred Caruso and
Burt Kimmelman
THE BEE FLIES IN MAY, Stephen Paul Miller
MAHREM: THINGS MEN SHOULD DO FOR MEN,
Edward Foster
REPRODUCTIONS OF THE EMPTY FLAGPOLE,
Eileen R. Tabios
DRAWING ON THE WALL, Harriet Zinnes
SERIOUS PINK, Sharon Dolin
BIRDS OF SORROW AND JOY: NEW AND SELECTED POEMS,
1970-2000, Madeline Tiger
ORIGINAL GREEN, Patricia Carlin
SHARP GOLDEN THORN, Chard deNiord
HOUSE AND HOME, Rochelle Ratner
MIRAGE, Basil King
NATURAL DEFENSES, Susan Terris
BRYCE PASSAGE, Daniel Morris
ONE THOUSAND YEARS, Corinne Robins
IMPERFECT FIT, Martha King
AFTER TAXES, Thomas Fink
NIGHT LIGHTS, Jane Augustine
SKINNY EIGHTH AVENUE, Stephen Paul Miller
SOMEHOW, Burt Kimmelman

Marsh Hawk Press is a juried collective committed to publishing poetry, especially to poetry with an affinity to the visual arts.

Artistic Advisory Board: Robert Creeley, Toi Derricotte, Denise Duhamel, Marilyn Hacker, Allan Kornblum, Maria Mazzioti Gillan, Alicia Ostriker, David Shapiro, Nathaniel Tarn, Anne Waldman, and John Yau.

For more information, please go to
http://www.marshhawkpress.org.